Metal Missives

A Tome of Lyrics, Poems and Anecdotes from the Hard Rockin' Days of Heavy Metal

By

James Shade

All text, lyrics and photos ©1987-2016

EPIC·AGE
MEDIA

"The Saga Unfolds..."

Table of Contents

Introduction

Oh, the yearning for the glorious days of heavy metal! You know you miss it. Sure today we might have death metal, black metal, and a few shows here and there by the Masters, but it's just not the same. Heavy Metal wasn't just a musical style, it was an era. Born out of the days of "classic rock" fans were looking for something heavier, something to take out their aggressions to, and heavy metal was it.

Though America was doing quite well, the cold war was taking its psychological toll, with a whole generation brought up to believe that the end of the world was nigh and that we were all going to die in a nuclear holocaust. So why not live it up and party while exorcising those dark demons of fear, paranoia and nihilism? While the rest of the world bickered over ideologies, we were united through music. Everyone embraced the long hair, the leather and torn jeans in this subculture, and it seemed that anyone could pick up a guitar and become a metal god. My friends and I were no exception. We started playing in 1989 at the tail end of this phenomenon, first in DARK FUTURE and 10 years later in ROGUE. By that point, the Berlin Wall had fallen and so the metal revolution sputtered and mutated into something else. But still we gave it a shot, trying to preserve some of that badass feeling that had been so prevalent in the past decade. Alas it was not meant to be, but it was a lot of fun trying.

I was the primary lyricist and bass player in both bands. And while we put out a debut EP, most of the songs we had written over the past 15 years didn't make it on there. So here is the complete collection for your enjoyment, for better or for worse. Some songs were written in high school and it's pretty obvious. The writing style got better as we went along but each song still had its own charm. Hope you like them. And maybe this little book will inspire you to dust off the old six-string and shred for a while...

Political

Though democracy has been trucking along nicely for a few centuries now, we are still far from the perfect system of government. Each one has its own perks and flaws, but it's the corruption and the pursuit of money and power that always screws it up in the end. I grew up pretty conservative, but have since mellowed my views. I will say this though: while America has accomplished some incredible things in its relatively short lifespan, we need to stop thinking of it, and ourselves, as the be-all-end-all society. There are MANY more nations out there and many different and better ways of doing things. Americans aren't the only people on the planet and we can't keep touting them as God's gift to the exclusion of all others. Live abroad for a while and you will see, there is so much more out there and so much that needs to be done and all humans need to work together to do it.

Practice session in the living room.

Enemy In Sight

Probably my second favorite song, as far as lyrics go. This is definitely one of those pieces that can be taken the wrong way by shortsighted, narrow-minded ignorant people. They get set off by trigger words without fully reading or understanding the context of the whole song. I have never been racist or anti-Semitic, but even now, though the entire concept should be considered a joke (as in "what the hell were we thinking?") these kinds of fears and attitudes still exist, after 10,000+ years of "civilization". Unbelievable. We started working on the music to this one, knowing we would take flak for it, but the band broke up before it was finished. So anyway, here is a little comment on the ugliest part of human nature.

Enemy In Sight

Man first came into the world
And soon his hatred was unfurled
He made war on his own kind
And thus his anger was defined
Forged the weapons he would wield
Armed the nations with sword and shield
Killed for power and killed for gold
His legacy would still unfold

Defined by war instead of peace
It's just the nature of our beast

Crush the Indians let them die
Burn the witches unto the sky
Gas the Jews and watch them choke
See Japan go up in smoke
Free the slaves to watch them fail
Don't let the communists prevail
Strike down the VC far from home
Then grind the Muslims into stone

There's no enemy in sight
We killed them all both black and white

Messages From Earth

Another unfinished little ditty on the state of our reality down here on this planet. Governments, religions and selfish people in general all doing the wrong thing when it's so easy to do the right thing. One type of suffering leads to another and another. Some would say we are evolved. I say "Ha!"; we still act like we did thousands of years ago. Only the tools are different.

Messages From Earth

You've got terror in the East
You've got the devil's bloody feast
You've got Heaven's sinning priest
All worshipping the Beast

Politician's lies
Devil in disguise
Killing us like flies
Everybody dies

Global warming trend
Never will it end
Help my planet mend
Or to Hell we will descend

<u>New World Order</u>

Too many people follow blindly and let the government, banks and other institutions get away with far too many things. Not enough people have the gumption to stand up for themselves and their rights, to speak up and speak out, to seek change in the world and their own personal situations. It is a terrible state of affairs to see our race behave and react like a bunch of sheep. In America especially, we have so many freedoms that are squandered, wasted and taken for granted. This needs to stop. If we ever want to grow, evolve and move forward within our society, we need to stand up and take charge!

New World Order

No lack of your conformity
See only that which you wish to see
Peace brings decadent complacency
Free will doesn't mean you're free

You can't change it, change what's done
No use fighting for that which can't be won
As your freedoms slowly turn to none
Who makes a difference? You are the one

The masses follow blindly in their haste
Liberty is not there for you to waste
Freedom: on this, our country, it is based
Could you imagine if all of this was erased?

Martial Law: it has lead us here
Anarchy: our leaders, they do fear
As we await the New World Order to appear
As Armageddon once again draws near

Peace talks, negotiations, no avail
Treaties of diplomacy, all shall fail
We see through your darkened veil
To the New World Order you must hail

Deadlocked, neither side will win
All for naught, stalemate once again
Nothing gained, nothing lost, time to begin
History repeats itself till the end

Psychological

Oh the mysteries of the human mind! Such a complicated maze of desires, whims, emotions, thoughts, fears and needs. It's our baser natures against our higher intellect and the result is something in between. Everything we do affects our life and others around us. But we are still so far from understanding even a fraction of what makes us tick and what is stored away in our unconscious minds. Is reality just an illusion?

My brother singing his guts out, probably a KISS song.

Spitting Image

I was pretty proud when I wrote this song, thinking myself eloquent in describing the battle each of us faces with our inner self, that little part of us that tells us we are a failure and will never amount to anything, to never try and to fear other people's opinions and judgment. We all have to conquer that negative little voice and overcome its influence if we are to ever accomplish anything. That being said, our singer thought it was just a song about me hating my mother!

Spitting Image

There is another you
There is another me
A part we cannot trust
To take control of us
Teller of untrue lies
Whispers in your ear
Blinder of your heart
Tears your dreams apart
Plays upon your inner fears
Succeed in nothing ever
Takes down your mask of hope
To the end of your rope

Where am I (I am here)
What am I (Always near)
Why this voice (This voice is true)
Who am I (I am you)

What the mirror does not reflect
(I spit on you)
Destroy your image of self respect
(I spit on you)
Deep within you cannot see
(I spit on you)
Destroy everything you want to be
(I spit)
I spit
(I spit on you)

Fight the censor, beat it down
Don't let the monster win
Stop him or he'll stop you cold
Do as you want not as you're told
Spit on me I spit right back
More than you'll ever be
Cut you out just like a knife
Guide myself through my own life
See me now what I have done
I listen to you no more
Free from your vicious grasp
Of you we've seen the last

<u>Nightmares</u>

The dreamworld is a scary place, since essentially anything and everything can happen there and it seems as real as our waking lives. In effect, it is an alternate reality that we carry with us every single day and are forced to endure and experience for hours every night. Things lurk there in our subconscious and come out to haunt you when you least expect it. Some people are lucky enough to have lucid dreams and know that it isn't "real" but most of us have to face this surreal landscape and hope that we wake up.

Nightmares

Blackout
Loss of consciousness
Say goodbye to reality
Prepare to face your inner self
You can't escape
For you are me
And now
With a silent scream
We fall deep into your mind
Prepare to face your darkest fears
As we break on through
To the other side
You walk
Into a nightmare
Your trip has just begun
Your insanity has you trapped
In your mind
There's nowhere to run
Shadows
Closing in on you
Blackened by your hate and lust
Haunting you and your inner thoughts
As your foolish pride
Turns to dust
Terror
In your reflection
The mirror it never lies
See yourself as you truly are
And watch
As your dignity dies

Nightmares, sinful
Nightmares, corrupt
This is a nightmare
But are you dreaming?

Into the Unknown

Aptly named, since I honestly don't remember the POV that I wrote this song from; it was so long ago. It's obvious that there are some demons or aliens involved and then perhaps a touch of the afterlife but it remains unclear. Still, ambiguity allows one to draw their own conclusions and ascribe their own meanings to works like this so...enjoy!

Into the Unknown

Messengers from the lost world
Have come to claim their right
A dark and forceful presence
Has joined with us tonight
From the bounds of forever
Absolute power theirs
Imposing their ungodly will
In forbidden prayers
Fear us, fear our ways
Face up, to the end
False life you have lead
Nothing left to defend
We shall redeem the faith
Your reign is at an end
As one we command
New world to begin

We journey alone
Into the unknown
Ascending the throne
Into the unknown

Destiny is at hand
Look close, you will see
Come now and join us
Let go and follow me
With open eyes release your fears
See now who you could be
Go forth into the world
You now hold the key

Your inner fires to be released
Set free to roam the world
Into this chaotic darkness
Your very soul is hurled
From this realm of chaos
Ultimate power achieved
All our hopes and visions
Our faith has been redeemed

Brain Static

It is obvious today that most people have become overly dependent upon their technological devices. I write this on a computer to upload it to the internet so you can read it on your phone. But we all got along just fine for thousands of years without the microchip, the TV, the radio, etc. Maybe we should give it a rest and do something useful like build amazing architectural marvels the way the ancients did WITHOUT electronics....

Brain Static

Hooked In
Plugged In
Wired In
Checked Out

Head Grip
Brain Chip
Mind Trip
Soul Slip

Upload
Download
Decode
Kill Mode

Connecting
Inspecting
Infecting
Rejecting

Techno
Info
Psycho
Mind Blow

High Gain
Low Gain
Migraine
Life Drain

Midnighter's Poison

Chances are you know someone who has been affected by alcoholism. Not a drinker myself but I do know a few folks who are. Then there are those who get addicted and it becomes a terrible sight to watch their lives fall apart around them because of this stupid beverage called "LIQUOR". So much lost potential, so many other things to spend your money on, so unhealthy for you and those around you. So sad.

Midnighter's Poison

Find me another
Way I can feel
What's left inside me
Will never heal

Never look back
When drinking it down
With this I am king
But where is my crown?

Midnighter's poison
The golden ale
It has become
The poor man's grail

Midnighter's poison
Down one more
One for the road
Should even the score

What can I do?
Where can I hide?
Swallow my poison
Swallow my pride

Midnight madness
Drives me insane
Sense of myself
I just can't regain

Midnighter's Poison
It drowns my mind
I cannot see
Cuz it makes me blind

Midnighter's Poison
It clouds my eyes
Somebody help me
Before I die

Empty a bottle
To fill my soul
I cannot stop it
It's out of control

One last toast
Before I go
Mindless in action
But I'll never know

Midnighter's Poison
Foolproof and pure
No one can save me
I've found my cure

Midnighter's Poison
Has done me in
It gave me power
But I let it win

Occult & Supernatural

One of the core topics that makes heavy metal what it is. So many bands with so many songs about demons, Hell, the devil, magic, the paranormal. This is what gave heavy metal its look and feel and what truly made it more interesting that your average music. It's also what got the genre into trouble on many occasions. But hey, no such thing as bad press, right? I personally am fascinated by this subject and have read many books on it. Do you believe?

Our promo flyer collage.

Mistaken Angel

Nowadays, thanks to numerous books and documentaries, the theory of ancient aliens is quite common. Of course, I wrote this one long before it became a popular viewpoint. The thought that aliens came down to Earth and were mistaken for holy or divine beings (which of course, for all intents and purposes, they were) is fascinating. To me, that would explain just about everything in every religion and shed light on almost every unexplained phenomenon in human history.

Mistaken Angel

Come to us
In our dreams
Come to us
How do we seem
Mistaken angel
In our eyes
Mistaken angel
Hear our cries

Down to earth
From the sky
Down to earth
Help us fly
Mistaken angel
From the past
Mistaken angel
We meet at last

Give us hope, give us fear
You are not what you appear
Give us pleasure, give us pain
What do you hope to gain?

Awakening

Lord of Night

Ah, the quintessential vampire story; how very cool...until it got WAY overdone. Honestly I can't stand vampires anymore simply because of what pop culture has done to them. Now they are everywhere and don't have nearly the kind of gravitas they used to. Really I think it's all some sort of sick sexual fantasy thing being played out, but to each his own. Anyway, this was written in the late 80's or early 90's, way before any of these teeny-bopper books, movies or TV shows were around.

Awakening

Lord of Night

I roam the streets at night
In the palest of moonlight
Waiting for my final day
Endless life of misery
Another cursed century
Before I pass away

Hunting in the blessed darkness
I prey upon the weak and harmless
Drain their lifeblood away
Led on by my constant thirst
Craving more than just the first
I seek more unwary prey

Life in Death
Immortal Soul
Life in Death
Undead Forever

Master of the darkest night
My death comes with dawns new light
King of my domain
My evil will shall never die
In my grave I'll never lie
Three hundred years my reign

Fire is burning in my glare
You are caught by my stare
Can't deny my deadly gaze
Death inside my eyes you see
Spellbound, you're no longer free
You shall do just as I say

Life in Death
Immortal Soul
Life in Death
Undead Forever

Follow as my willing slave
As I lead you to your grave
My command you shall obey
Hiding from my vicious wrath
Killing all within my path
For salvation you must pray

Hunger fills my long lost soul
Must have all that you hold
Must escape this inner pain
Quick and painless is your death
Breathing out your final breath
I live on while you decay

Life in Death
Immortal Soul
Life in Death
Undead Forever

Charlatan

Although it's couched in occult vocabulary, this song can apply to anyone who lies, steals, cheats, kills and generally has it out to screw over other people for his own gain. Don't let anyone sell you something you don't want or get sucked into a scheme that doesn't really reflect who you are, especially if you know it's wrong.

Charlatan

He is the one
Who will bring your demise
He's the fake healer
Who tells you the lies
An evil witch doctor
Charlatan his name
Spreading the fear
And chaos his game
No one to help you
You're at his command
You have been cursed
And you have been damned
A preacher of sin
This black hearted beast
Hear his name called
The hellbound priest

Charlatan has come
To corrupt your mind
He'll watch you die
And he'll leave you behind

The weak hearted spirit
He seeks to kill
Heed him not
Or he'll break your will

A wicked mystic
With a holy disguise
Passion for deception
Deep in his eyes
Converting your soul
Take your lifeblood away
Live for his sins
Till judgment day
He is your master
Get down on your knees
Now it's too late
For your pitiful pleas

Charlatan has come
With greed and hate
Don't give in or
He'll seal your fate

Night of the Witch

Actually, my first love and I kinda co-wrote this one together. She was big into Wicca at the time and we both had a pretty good wrangle on the lore and lingo so it was fun to throw it all out there. Here it goes more into the black magic aspect of things, which can be bad and dangerous. Of course, these types of songs were what gave pagans, Wicca and heavy metal an undeserved bad reputation.

Night of the Witch

Banished from the coven
Many centuries ago
Killing fellow members
For the master she bestows
Her familiars close at hand
Protecting their high priestess
From the corruption of a mortal
In this ritual of solstice

High priestess at the altar
Filled with rage and hate
Preparing for the ritual
A full moon she awaits
Conjuring kindred spirits
From the ground and from the air
Toll the magic handbell
For the mystics if you dare

Night of the Witch
(fire scrying, divination)
Night of the Witch
(crystal gazing, meditation)
Night of the Witch
(sacrificial incantation)
Night of the Witch

Sacred sword in one hand
A chalice held in the other
Chanting to the triple goddess
To the warrior, crone and mother
Obeying what the master said
Superstition still in mind
Seance done by candlelight
Satan's contract has been signed

Bound and gagged upon the ground
The victim's death grows near
Too scared to scream as time runs out
The air is filled with fear
The sword comes down with no remorse
The sacred rites are said
The invoking of the gods is done
The traitor now is dead

Warlock

Inspired by the movie of the same name, this one speaks of an evil and traitorous witch. I never finished it, which is fine because its sounds too much like CHARLATAN and NIGHT OF THE WITCH. Guess I was on a roll or stuck in a rut.

Warlock

I know thee
For I am Satan's son
I'll undo all you've wrought
And destroy creation

Three coins of copper
Between your teeth
To protect you from
The evil beneath

I live off your fear
I twist your words to lies
Meet my deadly stare
And lie bleeding from your eyes

Bad Guys

Having a strong and interesting central character is important to any story or piece of fiction. There are lots of nasty fellows out there, and some you may even empathize with or look up to. It's the whole anti-hero mystique that makes these guys cool. A sense of freedom and bucking the rules appeals to most people. Being a badass also helps.

Kevin dressed as a tourist for our Halloween debut.

Graverobber

Definitely my favorite song to play, I used this one in both bands. The two versions were even slightly musically different from each other. It was the song so nice we wrote it twice. A good solid rocker, it made it onto the ROGUE debut EP. I used to stand on top of my amp for this one and bang my head like crazy. It was just that good.

Graverobber

Midnight in the cemetery
Intruder stalks the grounds
Darkness in the night
Silence not a sound
Through the tombstones and ancient graves
Full moon lights the way
To the newly buried victims
The graverobber stakes his claim

The graverobber has come
To plunder and to steal
The graverobber has come
No remorse does he feel

No respect for the dead
He lives by desecration
The holy cross is naught to him
As he performs his violation
Souls are restless, seeking revenge
Lying helpless in their tombs
Crying out, eternal torment
Over them a curse does loom

The graverobber has come
To do his evil deed
The graverobber has come
To satisfy his greed

Nothing is safe, corpse or coffin
Mausoleums will be looted
Taking the riches of the dead
His evil is deeply rooted
One more eternal crypt
One last epitaph
Bids farewell to the sacred spirits
And leaves them to their wrath

Bounty Hunter

Yes, I have a large Boba Fett collection. I love the bounty hunter archetype, though I never watched that TV show. You get to hunt down bad guys but don't have to take any guff from superiors. You get to be your own boss, but you'd better know what the hell you are doing!

Bounty Hunter

Come and hear my sordid tale
Of a lifetime on the trail
Following the footsteps of my prey
While there's no one at my side
With my instincts as my guide
I'll be coming back to get my pay

Every time I take one down
Another bounty comes around
Thieves and killers never learn
But I'll be there to watch them burn

I'm a hunter
Hunt that bounty
I'll find you
You are the prize
I'm a hunter
Hunt that bounty
I'll get you
Dead or alive

When I track you from my ship
You know I'll never quit
Better find yourself another place to hide
Not a sense of right or wrong
It's the money that drives me on
I feel no fear as you do deep inside

Take them out or take them in
Either way I always win
Take them in or take them out
Either way you'll hear me shout

I'm a hunter
Hunt that bounty
I'll find you
You are the prize
I'm a hunter
Hunt that bounty
I'll get you
Dead or alive

Always ready for the attack
So you'd better watch your back
You'll not be the one to see my face
And as I close in for the kill
You can't bend my iron will
Now you're done and thus we end the chase

Round and round, again we go
Where you are, I always know
Run, run, run, you can't escape
You're going down, accept your fate

I'm a hunter
Hunt that bounty
I'll find you
You are the prize
I'm a hunter
Hunt that bounty
I'll get you
Dead or alive

Nightstalker

Back in the 80's, I was "lucky" enough to live in the same community that Richard Ramirez chose for his stomping grounds. One of his victims was just a few miles from my house! It was pretty crazy and people were freaked out for quite some time. They caught him not long after, but as everyone knows, it was AC/DC's fault...

Nightstalker

You are his next victim
And when it's your turn
You'll die like the rest
With your screams and squirms
You can try to run
But you cannot hide
He'll seek you out
And make sure that you've died
He'll show no mercy
This evil fiend
The devil's puppet
And demon seed

Hunting and killing
He preys on the fools
Hunting and killing
Insanity rules

He waits for night time
The time that is best
To rape and to kill
And bring unholy death
He hails to Satan
While Satan hails none
Simply promoting
The killing he's done

A knife in the gut
Your husband is dead
You're being raped
In your own private bed

He is the Nightstalker
He's stalking you

I am the Nightstalker
And I am stalking you

Assassin Extraordinaire

Assassins have always held a mystique for me; to be assigned a target; to study the victim; to plan for weeks in advance; to sit and wait for the perfect moment; to take his life without ever knowing what hit him. And no one ever knows it was you. It takes an extraordinary individual to master that art, and an even more extraordinary individual that can live with himself after.

Assassin Extraordinaire

Born in a hellhole
A child of war
A victim of society
He grew up mean
He grew up bad
Deadly as he could be
Master of weapons
Skilled in the art
Trained to kill on sight
None could escape
He hunted them down
Killing one each night

Killer, the assassin!

Perpetual threat
Evil at heart
Where next will he strike?
Kill, kill, kill
His only thought
Is to take your life
Infra red
In his sights
Do you live or die?
Paid to kill
Without a thought
Never asking why

The Demon Within

All of us are capable of atrocious acts if pushed too far. We like to think we are benevolent beings but the potential for evil is always there. Selfishness and envy are always just a step away, and it's a short ride from thinking about harming others to acting on that thought.

The Demon Within

A touch of sinful evil
An evil taste of sin
A hint of growing madness
From the corrupt soul within
A frenzied lustful demon
Under potent charm
Destroying his victims
Without bodily harm
A mystic binding master
Controller of their minds
Unnatural disasters
When he lurks behind

Beware the power
Avoid his grasp
Beware the power
See beyond his mask
Demon, within your mind
Demon, within your heart
Demon, within your soul
Demon, tears you apart

Crafty, sly and wicked
Serpent in the flesh
A renegade madman
A deviating wretch
Malevolent horrid monster
Deranged by his vice
A decadent creature
Born of fire and ice
A child of smiling fortunes
Always gets his way
Do not try to stop him
Or you will surely pay

The Dungeonmaster

Yes, I admit it: I played D&D for over 30 years. It was a lot of fun, I met a lot of interesting people and I even became a game designer because of it. In the game my primary role was that of the Dungeonmaster or DM, the teller of the story and the guy that lays out and enforces the rules of the game. So I guess this song is a tribute to myself...

The Dungeonmaster

Ruler of your fate
Cross him not
Stay away from hate
For he is your god

He makes the decision
Do you live or die
With any inquisition
He cannot tell a lie

A world of his own
To rule as he wishes
He stands alone
There are no conditions

A being of great power
In the palm of his hands
Awake at any hour
To adventure in his lands

He is the Dungeonmaster
To him you must listen
He can be a bastard
Or give you treasure that glistens

Man in the Dark

Looking back, I am not sure if I wrote this song about evil people in general or about Satan himself. Or maybe it was about some sort of demonic being with oodles of dark power. You decide!

Man in the Dark

I see a frightening figure
Dark shadows move aside
Carries the demon within him
I want to run and hide

The beasts have bled for him
He has had his fill
His soul has endless hunger
That no man can kill

The masses hear his word
They are the power
They sing his praises
At the witching hour

His dark and endless life
Will draw you in
Beware his hypnotic eyes
And the reaper's grin

Gliding on clouds of shadow
Don't turn your back
For everything he touches
Will turn to black

The night is his domain
From dusk until dawn
His legacy remains
His dark will goes on

A darker man I've never seen
He comes to you within a dream
He'll bring you flame, he'll bring you fire
He'll satisfy your soul's desire

Can he be real? Can he be right?
A silver tongue for your delight
Wild eyed serpent, wild eyed man
You'd better run while you can

The light he takes, the light he keeps
Too late now, you're in too deep
You hear him howl, you hear him scream
Now you know, he's not what he seems

Is the man in the dark, or is the dark inside the man?

Apocalyptic

Doomsday. Specifically, death by nuclear war. We all lived under that spectre for 50 years or so. It painted a bleak picture of our future, should we even survive to experience it. Made a great backdrop for a lot of songs and videos though. I like to think that all the songs we made to heighten awareness about this catastrophe also helped to avert it.

Rare shot of me shaved.

Dark Future

The name of our first band formed way back in 1989. This was to be our title track. Appropriately dark and scary it tells of current trends influencing future events. Greed and apathy will be our undoing so don't let people screw up this world for you and your descendants!

Dark Future

Another time, a different world
An era that has come
No one to help us, now it's too late
We have been undone

Far worse than today will be tomorrow
A world without hope, without sorrow
We're creating a dark future

A race against time to save the world
Destruction is thy fate
Destroyed by martyrs and evil men
Insane with greed and hate

Far worse than today will be tomorrow
A world without hope, without sorrow
We're awaiting the dark future

The sands of time are turning black
And are running low
Into the black and darkened void
This planet soon will go

Far worse than today will be tomorrow
A world without hope, without sorrow
We're all facing a dark future

The future is now and now it is dark
One last look at life
The four horsemen have come and as they ride
They laugh at our strife

Far worse than today will be tomorrow
A world without hope, without sorrow
We're all living the dark future

We're creating a dark future
We're awaiting the dark future
We're all facing a dark future!

Gamma World

A cheesy little song about a game. This is one of my all time favorite tabletop roleplaying games. At least, it was back in the 80's. So many new versions now, who can keep up?

Gamma World

Of chemical warfare and nuclear death
Enough has already been said
But what of the living, the one's that survived
The ones that envy the dead
The scourge of war and folly of men
Has transformed our mutated world
Into the dark oblivion of death
Their worthless lives will be hurled

Years of torture
Madness reigns
The earth is scorched and burned
Its survival of the fittest
This is Gamma World

A future of darkness, they live in this hell
Civilization is gone
Fighting to live yet wishing to die
Weeping with each new dawn
Screwing with nature and tempting the fates
The powers that be took a hand
But they must survive to carry on
The legacy of man

Gamma World
Only the strong survive in
Gamma World
No place to hide in
Gamma World
Our future is a
Gamma World
The final resting place
Of the human race
Is here in Gamma World

Rogue Trooper

Another song with material referenced directly from the board game and comic book of the same name. Pretty cool if you've never played it or read it. It's from the UK so you might have to hunt it down...

Rogue Trooper

Rogue Trooper
The savior of our land
In a dark future
A future made by man
With his helm and gunner
And bagman as his friends
He walks alone
Alone until the end

Rogue Trooper deals death
To Norts he sees
Sweetest revenge
For genetic infantry

A product of our science
And technology
Made from bits and pieces
Of others chemistry
He searches for the traitor
Of the quartz zone massacre
Undaunted, unfeeling
As he treks across Nu-earth

Through the scum swamps
And chemical jungles
The glass zone is not for me
From Microwave Mountain
To Timbuk-2
And on to Oman-3

Optimism

Can't be depressed all the time. Unless you are a Goth. Or emo. Who wants to live their entire life as a cynic? Yeah things always seem bad but you have to rise above it and find that silver lining. Make your own fun and happiness and try to impart that to others. Life is a cycle. What is absolute hell one day can turn into pure ecstasy the next.

Ticket Price $6		
Doors OPEN 8 PM	**ROGUE**	
	THURSDAY, FEBRUARY 4, 1999	
Concert Starts 9 PM	Club 369	1641 N. Placentia Ave., Fullerton 714 - 572 - 1816 21 & Over

Ticket from one of our early live shows.

The Talisman

Our power ballad, right smack in the middle of our debut EP. It says that the world is messed up right now but there is still hope if we put aside our grievances and work together to make the earth a better place. Sounds hippie but the music is pretty heavy and rockin!

The Talisman

Centuries of darkness
Our kingdoms are at war
Plagues of hatred and disease
Let us suffer no more
Our world in torment
Confusion and madness reign
Can we survive another day
In a world that has gone insane
We go in search of redemption
Please heal our weary souls
But no help on the horizon
Our pride has taken its toll
One chance to save ourselves
To take away the pain
We must undo what we have done
And erase this darkened stain
To find the key to salvation
This talisman of hope
Face up to our creation
And pray that we can cope
Not another day to pass
We must stand together
Save this planet from ourselves
And live in peace forever

Burning the Veil

A song written for a friend who was about to get married. She had doubts about her fiancé whom we all knew and liked but thought that they just weren't right together. I talked her out of it and she had the courage to break it off 2 weeks before the wedding. Sounds harsh but it saved both of them from making a big mistake. They are both happily married now to other people.

Burning the Veil

The past is passed
My future in my grasp
Never again to spend my days alone
To end my sin
To start my life again
To have someone that I can call my own

I'll be burning the veil
Burn my past all away
Burning the veil
See my night turn to day

I bring the ring
The holy angels sing
I'll never again regret what I have done
Now me is we
I am wed to thee
Forsaking others for my chosen one

Burn, burn away

To see the sea
Of sorrow there for me
Feel as though I'm lost without control
The end descends
My misery begins
Heart and mind torn from my very soul

I'll be burning the veil
Burn my past all away
Burning the veil
See my night turn to day

To dance the dance
Of lovers and romance
I'll find my way through this painful maze
The dawn is gone
The game goes on and on
I will prevail before my final days

Die Hard

Keep your spirits up, don't get discouraged. Go out into the world to kick ass and to take names! Don't be afraid to follow your dreams and achieve your goals in life. Don't listen to other people's negative criticism and don't be afraid to fail. Great song, just never got to put music to it.

Die Hard

As the time ticks away into the past
Be sure you're not the one to finish last
As the days pass turning into years
We must all face the future without fears
Beware the closing conspiracy
They'll try to bring down you and me
Don't give in or they'll succeed
This is how it was meant to be
Go out and take what they have to give
Perhaps you'll find out why you live
And as you deal with pain and strife
Remember just two words all your life

Die hard
In a world that will take you down
Society buries us without a sound
Die hard
In a world where we play for keeps
Die hard
Or forever hold your peace

Do not follow in another's steps
Make your own road to success
In a world where we're all alone
Find an existence to call your own
Now it's too late to go back
You've got to keep life right on track
We've got to learn from our mistakes
And just get back what life takes
And with that knowledge carry on
Through the years until we're gone
And while we're searching for the way
There's just two words I must say

Die hard
In a world that will take you down
Society buries us without a sound
Die hard
In a world where we play for keeps
Die hard
Or forever hold your peace

You can't avoid the coming wrath
Make the most of your chosen path
Don't waste your time or you will lose
You must decide before you choose
Don't let your life just fall apart
Or it'll be over before it starts
Don't let your problems get you down
They'd still be here if you weren't around
Don't let them stop you with their laws
You're willing to die hard for your cause
And as we leave you to your fight
Just these two words make you right

Die hard
In a world that will take you down
Society buries us without a sound
Die hard
In a world where we play for keeps
Die hard
Or forever hold your peace

Humorous

   I have always been the class clown. Just ask anyone how I bombard them with bad jokes and witticisms on a daily basis. Comedy comes easy to me. I love to watch it, read it and write it. But humor is a funny thing, different for everyone. Still, people need to loosen up and just laugh at life. It's the only way we can get back at the universe!

Front of our debut EP. A simple but effective logo.

Have No Fear

This was our show closer. Written about losers, it has a jaunty fun tune and it's pretty funny as long as you aren't the guy that we're singing about in the song! A good sing-along.

Have No Fear

Runnin' from the law
Tryin' to have it all
Take the easy way out
Have no fear, have no doubt

Low on cash
High on weed
Beer on your breath
No hope for tomorrow
The future brings your death

Make your move
Pick up chicks
Pleasures of the flesh
Care not for her feelings
Or the disease that you will catch

Have no fear
Have no fear

Wake up late
Cruise around
Losers have no fear
The whole world is a playground
All else disappears

Soon to die
Hell awaits
The time is drawing near
Never learned your lesson
And still you have no fear

Have no fear!

Old Man

No idea whatsoever.

Old Man

Old man Ebeneezer
Old man is a geezer
Old man is a wheezer

Old man in the kitchen
Old man's got an itchin'
Old man quit yer bitchin'

Old man in the shitter
Old man is a quitter
Old man, is he bitter?

Old man in his chair
Old man, is he bare?
Old man doesn't care

Old man's creaky bones
Old man's always home
Old man sleeps alone

Old man in the car
Old man in the bar
Old man's never far

Old man on the river
Old man aint a giver
Old man with no liver

Old man doesn't follow
Old man'd rather wallow
Old man, is he hollow?

Old man with a mutter
Old man in the gutter
Old man gives a shudder

Old man's never lead
Old man's lost his head
Old man, is he dead?

I Hate L.A.

For 21 years I suffered in that pit of hell they call lala land. My parents moved us there when I was just 9 years old and I wasn't able to escape until much later. By then the damage was done. I still have a few good friends there but I hope I never have to go back!

I Hate L.A.

I been livin' in a little old town called L.A., today
I been wantin' to move myself so far away, I pray
There aint nothin' there but the junkies and the hoes
Who can't wait to get some more powder up their nose
The surfers and the skaters just wanna hang their ten
While the gangers robbed my house and shot my dog again

I hate L.A.!

I came to Cali hoping to make it big, what a gig
I came to Cali and found only pigs, can ya dig?
If I wanna be famous I'll start a high speed chase
But I can't get away cuz there's traffic in my face
You can't be healthy if yer breathin' in the air
If there's nothin' in it for them, they don't even care

I hate L.A.!

I been lookin' for something good to say, about L.A.
You can't when they live in their filthy way, of decay
Give me a record deal, sign my dotted line
Sell me all your souls, make all your money mine
Let me play onstage, just five minutes more
Oh no! What happened? I've become a Cali whore!

I hate L.A.!

I want you to get out while you can, understand?
Forget about acting, forget about the band
I hope the earth cracks and they fall into the sea
But that's still not as bad as what they did to me
So when the day comes you will all hear me yell
See ya later Cali, I would rather live in Hell!!!

Who's Your Daddy?

Everyone seems to love this catchphrase for some reason, so I decided to give it a little kick. Puts a whole new spin on it, eh?

Who's Your Daddy?

In your room, you're all alone
Where no one can hear you moan
When you're lying on your bed
You're really messing with my head
You love to drive me up the wall
When you know I want it all
Yes, you're making me go mad
When I gotta have it bad

Hey little girl
Come to daddy
Hey little girl
Talk to daddy
Hey little girl
Run to daddy
Hey little girl
Who's your daddy?

If I could get just one more night
You'd give in without a fight
Better let me have my way
After that you'll want to stay
When your mom won't give it up
If she did it's not enough
Aint no sleazy one night stand
Gotta get it all I can

Hey little girl
Come to daddy
Hey little girl
Talk to daddy
Hey little girl
Run to daddy
Hey little girl
Who's your daddy?

Maybe one day you'll be rich
But for now you're daddy's bitch
Wanna see that little ass
Come on baby make it fast
I like to see you going down
When your mommy's not around
So when daddy is going deep
This little secret is ours to keep

Hey little girl
Come to daddy
Hey little girl
Talk to daddy
Hey little girl
Run to daddy
Hey little girl
Who's your daddy?

I'll get you my pretty...and your little sister too...

Grand Funk Roommate

Mark was a good friend of mine and a fellow Texan. He was always positive, funny, and encouraging. I was 11 years his junior but we stayed roomies for about 3 years. He had good intentions and great ambitions, but sometimes you just had to laugh at the guy. He was a good sport about it though. Unfortunately I lost track of the guy, so this is my tribute to him.

Grand Funk Roommate

In his little room
At the back of my place
There's a big bad Texan
With a goofy lookin' face
He's the life of the party
Though he's never invited back
Wild thing to his friends
His railroad's right on track

Grand Funk Roommate

His car says babe magnet
Though it's just a piece of shit
But get him on the green
And boy that man can hit
He's a rock and roll roommate
With Star Trek on the tube
He's got Eastwood in his closet
He's a rockin' golfin' dude

I think his name is Mark
He loves his American band
He thinks he is the king
But his girlfriend is his hand
He's not a steer or queer
He was just a normal guy
But then he got married
And his balls just said goodbye!

<u>Eclectic</u>

I tried to stay away from songs about relationships. Seems like 99% of musicians just want to whine about their girlfriends. Or their job. Or that their coffee is too expensive. I prefer to tell a story or, if possible, educate people. Don't just regurgitate the same old sappy sentiments. Give us something new or intriguing to wrap our brains around!

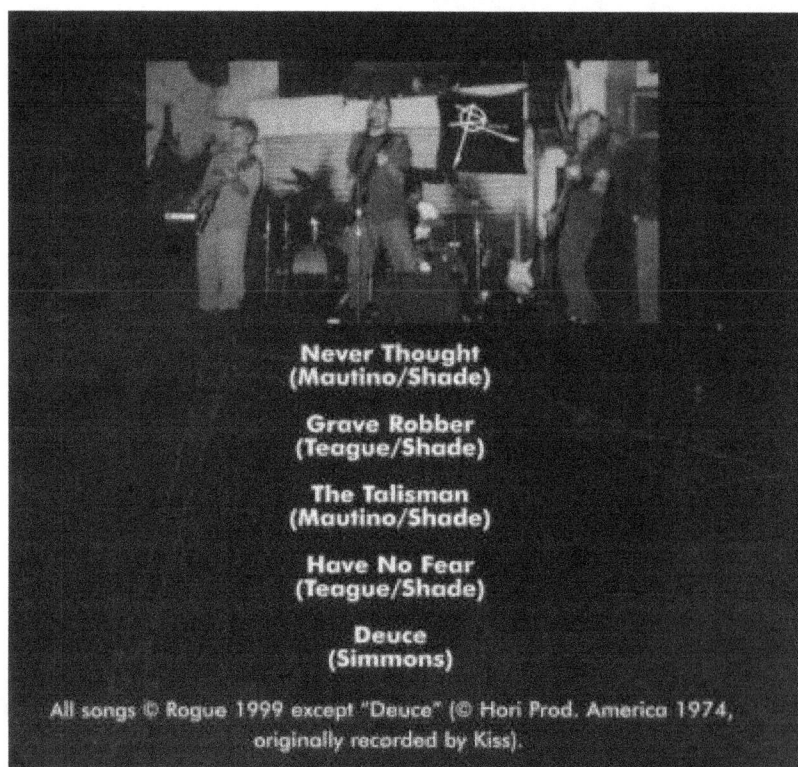

Never Thought
(Mautino/Shade)

Grave Robber
(Teague/Shade)

The Talisman
(Mautino/Shade)

Have No Fear
(Teague/Shade)

Deuce
(Simmons)

All songs © Rogue 1999 except "Deuce" (© Hori Prod. America 1974, originally recorded by Kiss).

Inside of our debut EP.

Killing For God

By far my most favorite song ever, musically and lyrically. I am a history buff and so I had to squeeze in this little ditty about the Crusades and what a catastrophic event it was. The music came out as a 7 minute epic with a nice bass solo right in the middle. We played it live but were never able to record it, as the band split before we could cut a second CD.

Killing For God

The soldiers march for glory
The soldiers march for their lord
The Saracens have come now
We must fight this heathen horde

Killing for God and my faith in His word
Killing for God and His wisdom unheard

They pillage for the army
The church's will to be done
They leave a trail of destruction
The battle's yet to be won

Killing for God when His words have been turned
Killing for God as His crucifix burns

Weather, disease and starvation
Matters not to the cause
To spread the word of the Christians
To violate their own laws

Two hundred years of fighting
The war has taken its toll
With mankind never learning
The path to saving its soul

Killing for God with His lessons unlearned
Killing for God and His wrath has been earned

Force

No secret as to what this song is about. Yes, I have been a Star Wars fan since I was 6 years old, way back in 1977. I thought this was a nice little tribute to and summary of the original brilliant trilogy.

Force

Fallen from the sky full of stars
Sent to find the son
Heralds of the New Republic
Empires day is done
Young man in search of his future
Goes on to win the fight
Old man from the barren desert
Leads him to the light
Two rogues on the run
Fight to save the day
One girl, beautiful princess
Struggles to lead the way
Dark lord, presence of evil
Grip tightened on the stars
Desperate battle for freedom
In a galaxy far
Beaten on the fields of ice
Force in full retreat
Hiding in the caves of stone
The enemy soon to meet
Chased down, betrayed by friendship
Hero bought and sold
Conflict of father and son
The truth is finally told
Rescued from the crime lord
Underworld pays the price
Return to keep the promise
To the master who is wise
Last chance for the Rebellion
To make their final stand
Triumph over the Empire
By this pitiful band
Father brought back from darkness
And his destructive course
They live together forever
In the light of the Force

Tales of the Spanish Main

Sadly, no one does concept albums any more. Not that there have been that many anyway, but I always liked the idea. For me, the main goal of a song is to tell a story and what better way to do that fully than to have an entire album dedicated to one topic. This one would have had a pirate theme, pirate artwork, a live pirate show...it would be awesome!

Tales of the Spanish Main

Long ago there lived a band of sea-faring thieves
They were born into the world to sail the seven seas
Raise the skull and crossbones high, the flag of villainy
They were bound to lead a life, a life of piracy

These wooden ships and iron men
In search of destiny
Found their final fate to lie
At the bottom of the sea

<u>Conquistador</u>

This would have been an epic song indeed, along the lines of Killing for God (see above). The conquistadors committed terrible atrocities all in the name of greed and glory. But had they not come this way and colonized the land would America even be here today? Not that anything could justify what they did but they certainly left their infamous mark on history.

Conquistador

No village or temple would be left to stand
Hundreds of Indians to die by his hand
Mayans and Aztecs to rule there no more
Time to die for the Conquistador

Rogue's Revenge

Kind of a weird possibly meaningless song, meant to be the title track for our second band. Actually I think we dropped the words and made it into an instrumental. No one does instrumentals anymore. I miss those.

Rogue's Revenge

It's too late
It's too late for you
Time for us
Time for us to do
What we want
Want to do to you
Move aside
We're coming through

It's over
It's done
Your time is at an end
It's over
It's done
This rogue will have revenge

We will rise
Rise above the rest
Unlike you
You have failed the test
See us now
See who is the best
No longer
Are we to be repressed

It's over
It's done
Your time is at an end
It's over
It's done
This rogue will have revenge

Rogue!

Swords of Steel

Another more generic, maybe even fantastic, historical tale. Not quite as good as Killing for God but still very visually evocative.

Swords of Steel

Once again it's the forces of good
Versus the armies of the night
Once again they meet to do battle
In what is to be the final fight
Battle hardened soldiers
Prepared to defend the land
Chaotic beasts surround them
The devil plays his hand

The dark brigade begins its charge
Ready to slaughter the steadfast men
The soldiers prepare to die in vain
As the dark brigade attacks once again
Screams of death and dying
The battle rages on
Will they live to see tomorrow
Will they live to see the dawn

March on, to conquest
March on, to victory
March on, to conquest
March on, to victory

Swords of steel, drawn and ready
Sunlight falling upon the blades
Swords of steel held high aloft
The din of battle never fades

The stench of blood and putrid smoke
Its foulness fills the air
The soldiers wish for death
In an unspoken prayer
But the tide of battle turns
The creatures start their rout
The soldiers all rush forward
With a bone chilling shout

Defeat is certain
Retreat is futile
Law and order reigns
The battle has been won

March on
March on
March on
March on!

Untitled

Another with potential for deep thought and meaning, scribbled onto a scrap piece of paper. Yet more unfinished lyrics...

<u>Untitled</u>

Strange this compulsion
Fed by the anger inside me
Filled with emotion
Blinded by it, I cannot see
The devil's hand to guide me
The devil's will inside me

Random collage shot.